SUDDEN DEATH

ILLUSTRATED HISTORY OF WORLD CUP FOOTBALL AS A MYSTERY THRILLER
Part One

Arun & Maha

CricketSoccer

This paperback edition first published in 2018
CricketSoccer
www.cricketsoccer.com

Copyright ©Arun and Maha

The right of Arun and Maha to be identified as the authors of this book has been asserted by them in accordance with the Copyright, Design and Patent Acts 1988

ISBN 978-1732522602

All rights reserved. No part of this publication may be reproduced, transmitted, or stored in a retrieval system, in any form or by any means, without permission in writing from CricketSoccer

To
Sushmita and Coco

without whom
this collaboration
would not have happened

Acknowledgements

The authors would like to express their sincerest thanks to the whole team associated with CricketSoccer, namely Tim Stannard, Faisal, Vieri Capretta, Paco Polit, Javed Ikbal, Avijit Sen and others, for their continuous support.

They would like to thank Meghana of Shadow Editing Services for her excellent work with the manuscript. Special gratitude to Uli Hesse and Kashinath Bhattacharjee for helping out with their immense knowledge. And finally, many thanks to Tanoy Dutta for his constant faith and encouragement.

Introduction

The history of the World Cup is full of riddles and mysteries. For instance, what happened to the original trophy, the Coupe Jules Rimet? If you scour the internet, you'll read that it was stolen from the headquarters of the Brazilian FA, melted into gold bars and sold. But this is probably nonsense. Pedro Berwanger, the policeman in charge of the investigation, pointed out that the cup as such was a lot more valuable than the gold it was made of. Which is why some people think that the trophy now sits on the shelf of a ruthless collector in some secret location.

Speaking of vanished objects, where is the ball from the 1954 final? The German FA claims it's in their shiny, large museum, but this is highly doubtful. The referee, William Ling, took possession of the ball after the game and for all we know, he still had it when he emigrated to Canada where he died in 1984. Most experts suspect the ball in the museum is from the semi-final or even just a ball used for training.
Men have vanished as well. Where is Joe Gaetjens, the man who scored one of the most famous World Cup goals of all time – the USA's 1-0 against England in 1950? In July 1964, he was arrested by the secret police in his native Haiti. That's the last we heard of him.

There are also numerous less sinister mysteries. What did Materazzi really say to Zidane in 2006? What did really happen to Ronaldo ahead of the 1998 final? Or what about the Mexican wave? We associate it with the 1986 World Cup, hence the name, but there is compelling evidence it was invented in 1981 and by a single man – an American called George Henderson. It should be called the Californian wave, really.
So it was about time that someone sat down to tell the story of the World Cup through riddles and mysteries. Or rather, through a mysterious man who speaks in riddles.

Arun (Arunabha Sengupta) has already proved he is up to the task with a novel in which none other than Sherlock Holmes solves a cricket case. But now, in this book by Arun and Maha, one man's brains are not enough – it takes an entire team of football experts and lovers to solve the riddles mentioned above and help save FIFA's money to ensure the next World Cup can be staged.

It means the book works on many levels. You can read it as a thriller or as a history book – or even as a puzzle book. Can you solve the riddles before FIFA's team can? Could I? Well, that must remain a mystery.

Uli Hesse

The Line up

Herr Fassler : Chief Financial Officer of FIFA, compulsive worrier

Mike Templeton: Football Historian, nibbler nonpareil

Sonja Bjarkardóttir: Genius code breaker, short-lipped and sassy

Javier Hernandez: Interpol Agent, cucumber-calm man of the world

FIFA is in turmoil. On the eve of the 2018 World Cup, the tournament is on the verge of falling through as a crazy football fan holds the organisation at ransom. It is up to these four curious characters to save the day.

Answer the question --- if incorrect the balance will be transferred to an untraceable account. You have 1 minute. Your time starts now.

Beverage for a different game/To the prologue did it lend its name.

_ _ _ _ _ _

Thought as much.
This was very very simple and you messed up.

All your funds are now wired to an untraceable account in the Caymans or Switzerland...You have to enter the correct answer to proceed further.

... And then we will play a game of 20 questions

- The game will be played in 5 rounds
- Each round will have 4 questions based on the past World Cups
- At the end of each round, if you get all 4 questions correct, 20% of your funds will be transferred back to your account. You will be able to proceed to the next round.
- Any wrong answer ends the game. However, the funds already transferred, will remain with FIFA. The rest of the money will be lost.

- Questions will be asked every 2 hours
- Time permitted to answer each question is 15 minutes
- Timer will start automatically on your laptop

- The only way to recover your money and ensure the World Cup goes on exactly as planned is to answer all my questions correctly.
- We start tomorrow at 10 AM.
- Assemble all the required help by then

  I am sick and tired of football-ignorant buffoons running the game.

10 : AM
Ding !

A cross that could not win the cup/ Not for a header, not that far up

— — — — —

1930 Uruguay

Time had come to throw football to the world. It was not England and the rest any more.
FIFA had existed from 1904.

Football had been contested in the Olympics since 1908.

But by 1929, FIFA decided on a trophy of their own. Professionalism had spread way further than the boundaries of the Games.

Four Scandinavian countries and Estonia disagreed. But the other 25 voted for a tournament in 1930.

In the midst of the Great Wall Street Crash. In the face of Global Depression.

Where would it be played? Sweden, shortly after voting against the World Cup, wanted to host. So did Italy, Spain and Holland.

But who were the superpowers of the football world?

Uruguay. With stern defence and some spectacular inter-passing. They had triumphed in the 1924 and 1928 Olympics. Only neighbours Argentina, their Copa America rivals, were worthy challengers.

And they clinched the hosting deal by agreeing to bear the cost of travel and accommodation of every visiting team. After all it was the centenary of their independence. They even promised to complete their main stadium in time. They were still building it when the final was played

The first World Cup to be held in Montevideo, according to some European reportage "A third world shanty town."

European countries were loathe to travel across an ocean. Hungary, Italy, Austria, Germany, Spain ... the major powers ... did not participate. England and Scotland were not members of FIFA. France, Belgium and Yugoslavia did travel. As did Romania. The German speaking King Carol ensured that Romanian footballers got on the boat.

Group Matches

Group 1

Team	Chile	France	Mexico	GF	GA	Pt
Argentina	3-1 (2-1)	1-0(0-0)	6-3 (3-1)	10	4	6
Chile		1 0 (0 0)	3 0(0 0)	5	3	4
France			4-1(3-)	4	3	2
Mexico				4	13	0

Group 2

Team	Brazil	Bolivia	GF	GA	Pt
Yugoslavia	2-1 (2-0)	4-0(0-0)	6	1	4
Brazil		4-0 (1-0)	5	2	2
Bolivia			0	8	0

Group 3

Team	Romania	Peru	GF	GA	Pt
Uruguay	4 0 (4 0)	1 0(0 0)	5	0	4
Romania		3-1 (1-0)	3	5	2
Peru			1	4	0

Group 4

Team	Paraguay	Belgium	GF	GA	Pt
USA	3-0(2-0)	3-0(2-0)	6	0	4
Paraguay		1-0 (1-0)	1	3	2
Belgium			0	4	0

Highlights:

Romania vs Peru was played in front of just 300 people

Brazil capped 10 new players against Yugoslavia

Semi Finals

Argentina and Uruguay galloped through the semi-finals with identical routs.

Argentina 6 (1) USA 1 (0)

In a game of rough tackles, American trainer Jack Coll entered to attend to a player, dropped a bottle of chloroform from his medical bag and had to be led off in a trance.

Uruguay 6 (3) Yugoslavia 1 (1)

Uruguay supposedly scored their third goal when a ball went out of play and was kicked back by a policeman in uniform

Final

Uruguay 4 (1) Argentina 2(2)

As tensions ran riot, referee John Langenus had several stipulations.

68,346 people crowded into the stadium, many of them from Argentina, who had crossed the River Plata, that separated the two countries. Luis Monti, the Argentinian midfielder, received death threats from both countries. He remained in a state of panic throughout, and migrated to Italy within a few years.

There was also the Uruguayan coalition government, tottering on a coup by military dictatorship. Langenus ordered two balls for different halves, manufactured in the two different countries. He also demanded a quick escape route plan to get back to his ship as soon as the game was over.

Even as the Uruguayans celebrated, Langenus sprinted to his waiting boat as soon as he blew the final whistle.

Highlights:

Juan and Mario Evaristo of Argentina became the first brothers to play in a World Cup Final.

Juan Jose Tramutola, the Argentinian 'technical director' was just 27 when his team played the final.
Alberto Suppici, his Uruguayan counterpart, was just four years older at 31.
Eight Argentinians never played for the national side again
One Uruguayan supporter was killed during celebrations.
The Jules Rimet trophy, named after the 3rd FIFA President, was designed by Abel Lafleur and made of gold-plated sterling silver on a white/yellow marble base. It cost 50,000 Swiss Franc.

Top Scorer and Best Player: 1930 Uruguay

This 25-year-old forward made his international debut for Argentina in the nation's second World Cup match against Mexico. He got his opportunity when preferred striker Roberto Cherro dropped out of the game due to an anxiety attack.

Argentina won the game 6-3 with Stábile scoring a hat-trick.

This was long thought to be the first ever hattrick in World Cup football, until FIFA ruled in 2006 that Bert Patenaude, of United States, had been the pioneering hat-trick scorer, against Paraguay, two days before Stábile. Thankfully Stábile passed away 40 years before this change of mind.

In the next game, Stábile scored twice against Chile in a 3-1 win.

He scored twice more against United States in a 6-1 semi-final win.

In the final, his goal put Argentina 2-1 ahead against hosts Uruguay. That was the score at half time. However, Uruguay scored thrice in the second half to win 4-2.

Stábile thus finished the inaugural World Cup as the top scorer, with 8 goals from 4 games. He never played for Argentina again, thus finishing with the record of scoring in every game he played for his country.

He later played for Genoa, scoring another hat-trick on debut against Bologna. Further down the line he turned out for Napoli and Red Star Paris.

Still later, as manager, he guided Argentina to six Copa America wins.

José Nasazzi, defender and captain of the World Cup winning Uruguayan side, was adjudged the best player of the tournament.

Congrats!
You now proceed to the next question of this round

1934, Italy

Italy, 1934. Fascist state, one-party rule, brownshirt gangs, informers, state murder, imprisonment without trial. That was where the second World Cup was hosted.

The tournament followed a knock out format. Uruguay did not participate, becoming the first and only team that did not defend the Cup. Brazil and Argentina sailed eight thousand miles to play one match each.

With the political climate dangerously fascist, the Italians, coached by authoritarian Vittorio Pozzo, desperately wanted to win. Benito Mussolini himself, wearing his famous sailor's cap, appeared in the Stadio Nazionale, Rome, to watch his *azzurri* in action.

The Fascist government stood ready to pick up the cheque for the tournament. It was a prime propaganda tool.

Italian team of 1934 performing the fascist salute. The closest rivals of Italy were the Austrian Wunderteam, coached by Hugo Meisl.

First round			
Italy 7(3) United States 1 (0)	Czechoslovakia 2(0) Romania 1 (1)	Germany 5 (1) Belgium 2 (2)	Austria 3 (1) France 2(1) Full Time (1/1)
Spain 3(3) Brazil 1(1)	Switzerland 3(2) Holland 2(1)	Sweden 3(1) Argentina 2(1)	Hungary 4(2) Egypt 2(1)
Second Round			
Germany 2 (1) Sweden 1 (0)	Austria 2(1) Hungary 1 (0)	Italy 1(1) Spain 1(0) Replay Italy 1(1) Spain 0(0)	Czechoslovakia 3(1) Switzerland 2 (1)

Pozzo helped himself to a number of South American internationals. They were eligible for national service for Italy. Pozzo's logic was "If they can die for Italy they can play for Italy"

Atilio José Demaría and Luis Felipe Monti played for Argentina in the 1930 World Cup and Italy in the 1934 edition.

Semi Finals
Italy 1(1) Austria 0(0)
There was a deluge in Milan preceding the match. Italy was happy to leave pools of water on the pitch to counter the Wunderteam's style of play.

In the 19th minute, Enrique Guaita scored from a ball spilled by Austrian goalie Peter Platzer after a sliding challenge by Giuseppe Meazza.

Czechoslovakia 3 (1) Germany 1 (0)
The short passing game of the Czechs won the day. However, the German goalkeeper Willi Kress was blamed for two of the goals. But, that takes nothing away from the brilliance of Nejedlý's hat-trick.

The German coach Otto Nerz later died in the Sachanhausen concentration camp.

3rd Place Final
Germany 3 (2) Austria 2 (1)
On this day the Germans stopped the Wunderteam. By the time the next World Cup would be played, their country would wipe Austria off the map.

Final

Italy 2 (0) Czechoslovakia 1 (0). 1-1 after full time.
It was goalless with 20 minutes left when Antonín Puč had to be carried to the sidelines after being on the wrong side of a rough tackle. A flask of ammonia was waved under his nose. Two minutes later, he scored the first goal. (Example of drug use?)

Italy equalised with minutes to spare. In the extra time, Pozzo asked Schiavio and Guaita to switch positions, and five minutes later Schiavio netted the winner.

It is said that Meazza's handball went unnoticed in the move that resulted in the clinching goal. The referee, Sweden's Ivan Eklind, was supposedly seen with Mussolini before the final.

Highlights:

The centre forward and centre half of Italy had a fractious relationship. Pozzo's remedy was forcing them to be roommates.

Monti became the only player to play in two World Cup finals for different teams. This time he did not receive any death threat

Top Scorer and Best Player : 1934, Italy

Oldřich Nejedlý played all his career for Sparta Prague. Yet, in some curious way of football and life he remained forever connected to Italy. In the 1934 World Cup held in that country, Nejedlý was voted the third-best footballer in the tournament and the joint top-scorer with four goals alongside Angelo Schiavio and Edmund Conen. This included two goals in the semi-finals against Germany which Czechoslovakia won 3-1. The third goal was credited to Rudolf Krčil.

In 2006, however, FIFA recognised Krčil's goal to be Nejedlý's, making the inside left the undisputed top scorer of the tournament and also awarding him a hat-trick in the semi-final.

He also scored two more goals in the 1938 World Cup in France, before a broken leg ended his tournament and international career.

The only blot in his World Cup journey was perhaps hitting over the bar in the final in 1934, when a goal would have put the Czechs 2-0 up against Italy.

Curiously, he passed away in 1990 when the World Cup was being played ... once again in Italy.

The versatile Italian forward **Giuseppe Meazza** was adjudged the best player of the 1934 tournament.

Not only did Meazza score memorable goals, he masterminded Italy's triumph in the semi-final over the Austrian Wunderteam on a hideously muddy San Siro pitch.

He hobbled through most of the final, after receiving a rough tackle early on, but played a crucial role in crafting the deciding goal.

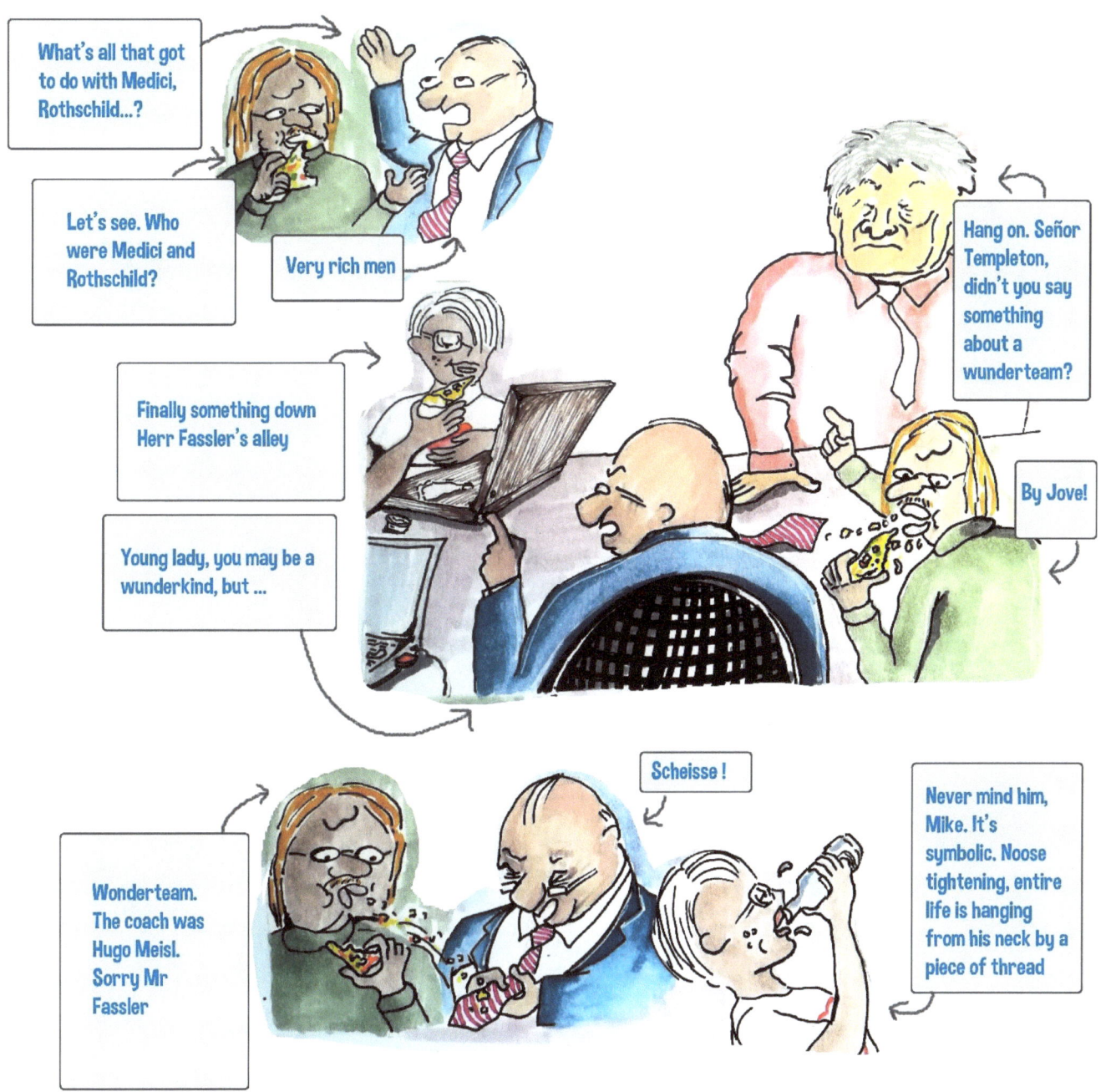

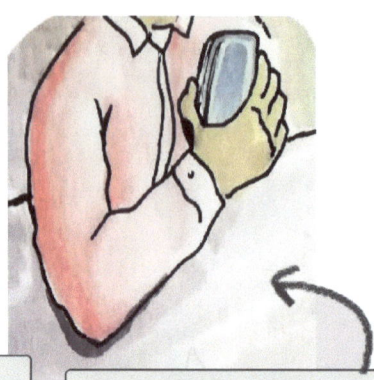

1938, France

The teams fought for the Cup but the World was in turmoil.

Austria, the land which had produced the Wunderteam, was swallowed by the German *Anschluss*. Czechoslovakia, the finalist of 1934, played in the tournament but were soon to be occupied by the Nazis. Spain suffered from civil war.

Latin American presence was limited. Uruguay stayed away, still sulking from the absence of European countries in 1930. Argentina were not happy that France had been granted the World Cup they wanted to host.

And England, still outside FIFA, did not accept the invitation to take the place of Austria.

So, teams that participated included Cuba and the Dutch East Indies (colonised Indonesia).

In their opening match Dutch East Indies goalkeeper brought a fat faced doll to the pitch, but it could not put a hex on the Hungarians who won 9-0.

Playing an early version of Catenaccio, Switzerland ousted Germany in the first round, in spite of the latter loading the side with Austrian greats. It became part of Swiss and football folklore.

First round			
Switzerland 1 (1) Germany 1 (1) Replay: Switzerland 4 (1) Germany 2 (2)	Cuba 3 (1, 2) Romania 3 (1, 2) Replay: Cuba 2(0) Romania 1(1)	Hungary 6 (4) Dutch East Indies 0 (0)	France 3 (2) Belgium 1(1)
Czechoslovakia 3(0,0) Holland 0 (0,0)	Brazil 6 (3,4) Poland 5(1,4)	Italy 2 (1,1) Norway 1(0,1)	
Second Round			
Sweden 8(4) Cuba 0(0)	Hungary 2(1) Switzerland 0 (0)	Italy 3(1) France 1(1)	Brazil 1(1,1) Czechoslovakia 1(0,1) Replay: Brazil 2(0) Czechoslovakia 1(1)

Born of a Russian father, Eugen Wallaschek, who scored the first goal in the 4-2 win in the Switzerland-Germany replay, did not get a Swiss passport until eight days after the game.

Alois Beranek, referee in the Italy-Norway match, was yet another Austrian representing Germany.

The Brazil-Czechoslovakia quarter final, eventually decided through replay, was an all-out rough tackling war.

After the Sweden-Cuba match, French journalist Emmanuel Gambardella said: "Up to five goals is journalism. After that it becomes statistics."

Semi Finals
Hungary 5(3) Sweden 1(1)
The Hungarian *Kombinationsmaschine* was irresistible. It did not help Sweden that Sven Jacobsson opened the proceedings with an own goal.
Italy 2 (0) Brazil 1 (0)
In perhaps the worst selectorial blunder, Leônidas de Silva, top scorer in the World Cup, was left out of the Brazilian team. However, some claim that he had not recovered from the Brazil-Czechoslovakia war. Giuseppe Meazza, slower and clumsier due to his notorious nocturnal activities, scored the second goal from penalty.
3rd Place Final
Brazil 4 (1) Sweden 2 (2)
Leônidas was back, and there was no stopping Brazil. Not quite… they were two down before the first half-hour. But come back they did.
Final
Italy 4 (3) Hungary 2 (1)
Italy proved too quick, their 'ramparts keeping out the Danube'. Michele Andreolo, the Uruguayan import playing as the centro mediano, kept a check on György Sárosi, the Hungarian centre-forward. And then there was Silvio Piola with his two goals.

At the end of the game Meazza wept. Pozzo stood there, dazed, while water poured from the trainer's bucket into his shoes.

Mussolini received the winning team, but was bareheaded this time. In contrast, the footballers wore sailor caps.

Top Scorer and Best Player 1938, France

"He was as fast as a greyhound, as agile as a cat, and seemed not to be made of flesh and bones at all, but entirely of rubber... He shot from any angle and any position, and compensated for his small height with exceptionally supple, unbelievable contortions, and impossible acrobatics."

Was Leônidas de Silva the inventor of the bicycle kick? One can never be sure. But he excelled at it.

Leônidas de Silva

They called him 'Diamant Negro' (Black Diamond).

In 1939, *Lacta* purchased this sobriquet from him to launch their brand of chocolate. His other nicknames were 'Magia Negra' (Black Magician) and 'Rubber Man'.

In the macabre match against Poland, which Brazil won 6-5, Leônidas scored thrice. The muddy pitch tore the sole of his boot. He tried to play in his socks but the referee ordered him to put his footwear back on.

In a brutal quarter-final against Czechoslovakia, Leônidas scored in a 1-1 draw before limping off the field. In the replay he scored the equaliser before Brazil won 2-1. And then the team management rested him in the semi-final defeat against Italy.

In the third-place play-off against Sweden Leônidas was back, named captain, and scored twice in the 4-2 victory. He was the top-scorer with seven goals and also named the best player of the tournament.

Leônidas enjoyed a long career, playing his last seven years for São Paulo. His off the field activities were also as interesting.

In 1941 he was jailed eight months for forging a certificate exempting him from army service. Later he managed São Paulo, was a radio commentator and worked as a private detective.

Leônidas died aged 90, after a long bout against Alzheimer and diabetes.

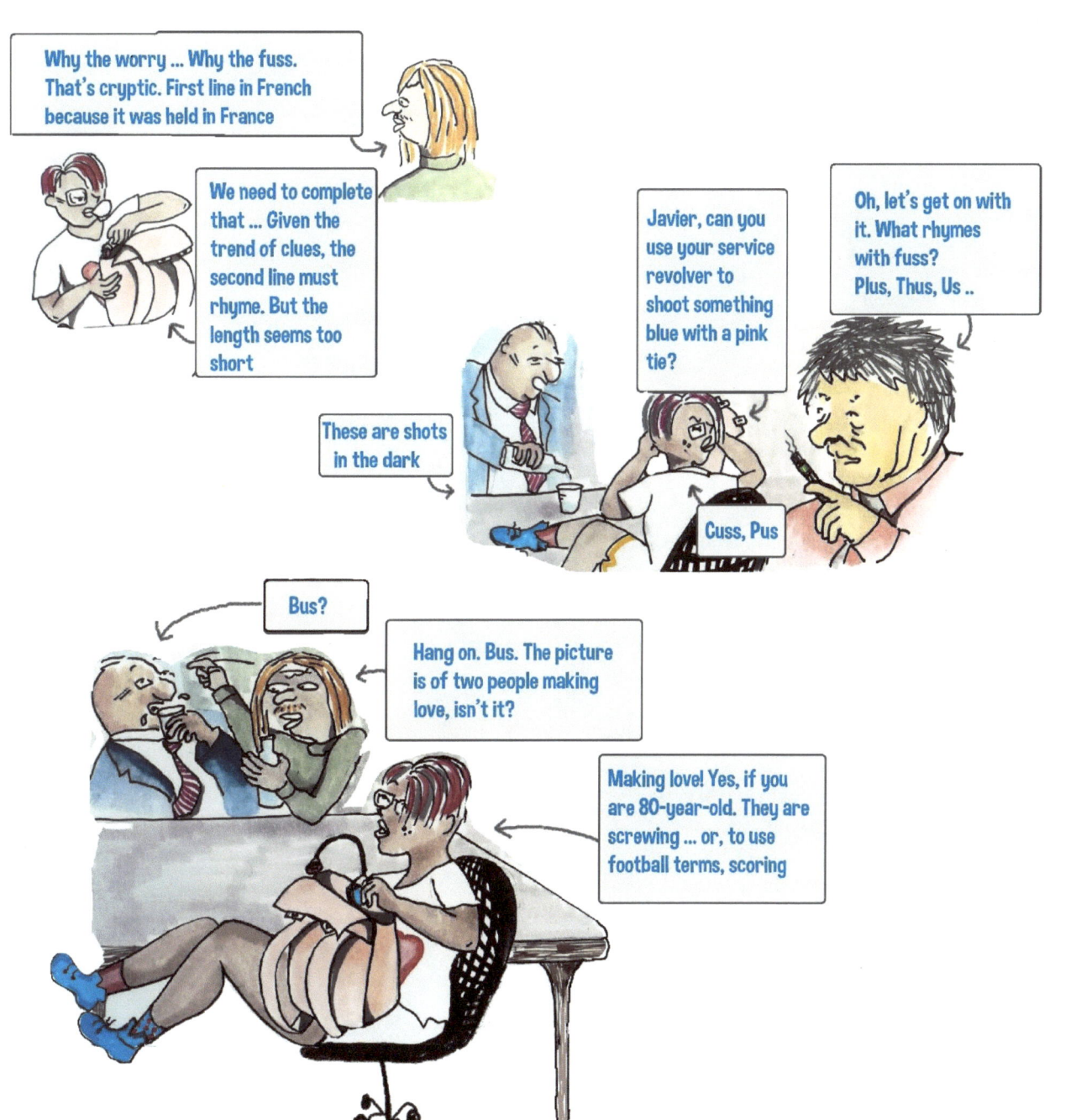

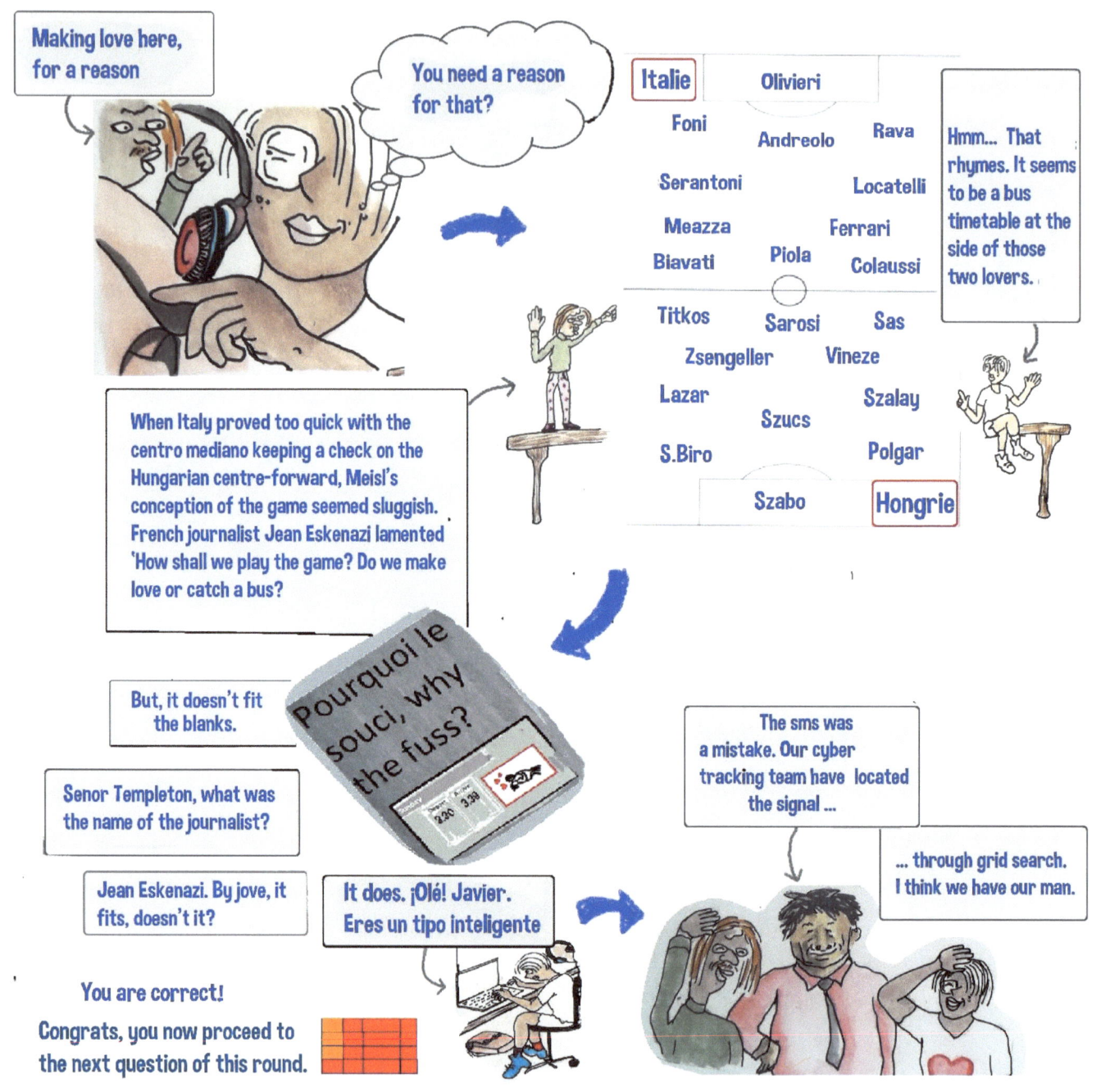

> Mmm...that's a real cool 'Clue Delivery' idea!

> What took place in 1950? Let us recall.

1950, Brazil

The War was over. Finally, once again, the entire world could focus on a ball being kicked around.

The tournament was held in Brazil. Many of the European sides withdrew, some citing valid reasons and others offering bizarre ones. It was Argentina's withdrawal that hurt the most, the Latin American giants refusing to participate in a tournament held virtually at their doorstep.

On the positive side, England competed in a World Cup for the first time.

It was a tournament that did away with the knock-out format. Four groups were drawn up, and as the withdrawals struck, they were not reorganised. It left Uruguay and Bolivia as the sole members of a farcical Group 4.

The groups were not divided into zones either. Hence, the teams had to travel through the length and breadth of the huge country to play their matches.

There was no title round, with the four group winners going into a final pool and playing another league.

The Maracanà stadium was being built, with twice the capacity of Wembley. But it was still work in progress when the teams arrived. By the time the match, which was the virtual final, was played, and 200,000 people thronged in, it still looked like a construction site.

First Round

Group 1

Team	Yugoslavia	Switzerland	Mexico	GF	GA	Pt
Brazil	2-0(1-0)	2-2(2-1)	4-0 (1-0)	8	2	5
Yugoslavia		3-0 (0-0)	4-1(2-0)	7	3	4
Switzerland			2-1(2-0)	4	6	3
Mexico				2	10	0

Group 2

Team	England	Chile	USA	GF	GA	Pt
Spain	1-0(0-0)	2-0(2-0)	3-1 (0-1)	6	1	6
England		2-0 (1-0)	0-1(0-1)	2	2	2
Chile			5-2(2-0)	5	6	2
USA				4	8	2

Group 3

Team	Italy	Paraguay	GF	GA	Pt
Sweden	3-2(2-1)	2-2(2-1)	5	4	3
Italy		2-0(1-0)	4	3	2
Paraguay			1	4	1

Group 4

Team	Bolivia	GF	GA	Pt
Uruguay	8-0(4-0)	8	0	2
Bolivia		0	8	0

Highlights:

The inaugural match, between Brazil and Mexico at the Maracanà, saw 5000 pigeons released and a 21-gun salute. The latter did not really help the new structure with its plaster drying.

In the Yugoslavia-Switzerland encounter at Independencia, floodlights were switched on for the first time in a Cup match.

The Brazil-Switzerland match was played in São Paulo. The Brazilian coach, Flávio Costa, considered the Swiss to be non-contenders and brought in a lot of São Paulo players, presumably to please the crowd. After the 2-2 draw, the crowd almost lynched him.

Dent McSkimming of the *St Louis Post-Despatch* was in Brazil on holiday and thereby the only American reporter in the USA-England match which ended 1-0 in favour of the former. An editor in London thought the scoreline was a misprint for 10-1.

Three players turning out for the USA, Joe Maca, Ed McIlvenny and Joe Gaetjens, were supposedly ineligible to play for them. Gaetjens went back to playing for Haiti by the time of the next World Cup qualifiers, and in 1964 was murdered by the Tonton Macoutes.

Final Pool

The format of the tournament was to play a round-robin league with the final pool, comprising of the winners of each group.

Yet, when Uruguay played Brazil in the final match at the Maracanà, it was as good as the title round.

Brazil, having trounced Sweden 7-1 and Spain 6-1, needed just a draw to win the World Cup.

They took 30 shots at the goal, and in the 47th minute took the lead as well. But the wall of Uruguayan defenders stood firm, shadowing the great Brazilian frontline. Obdulio Varela, the skipper, stayed back to help Eusebio Tejera mark the dangerous Ademir. Goalkeeper Roque Máspoli had the game of his life, and the attacks along the wings broke through the Brazilian defence. Juan Schiaffino equalised and Alcide Ghiggia, beaky and moustachioed, made it 2-1.

It was a result that would haunt the Brazilians for generations.

Team	Brazil	Sweden	Spain	GF	GA	Pt
Uruguay	2-1(0-0)	3-2(1-2)	2-2(1-2)	7	5	5
Brazil		7-1(3-0)	6-1(3-0)	14	4	4
Sweden			3-1(2-0)	6	11	2
Spain				4	11	1

Highlights:

In the match against Sweden, Ademir scored three goals. One of them was a bicycle kick after flipping the ball up with another foot. Another, supposedly, was with the ball trapped between his ankles as he jumped over the keeper.

Schubert Gambetta played for Uruguay against Sweden and Brazil. In a curious musical link, representing the country against England in 1977 was Beethoven Javier.

The first goal conceded by Spain against Brazil was earlier credited to Ademir, but later it has been agreed that it was an own goal by José Parra.

Danilo Alvim Faria, the great Brazilian centre half, supposedly attempted suicide after the Cup. He was not successful, but a couple of Brazilian supporters were.

Moacyr Barbosa, the Brazilian goalkeeper, was offered the goal posts of the final game 13 years after the World Cup. He invited his neighbours to a barbeque and torched the souvenirs.

Top Scorer and Best Player 1950, Brazil

He was lightning quick, could produce blistering cannonball shots with both feet and was superb in the air. His incredible dribbling skills, changes of tempo, phenomenal acceleration and deceptions carried out at explosive speed were topped off with sublime finishing. Through his career he bore the nickname Queixada (jaw) because of his eye-catching underbite.

With Thomas Soares de Silva (Zizinho), and Jair da Rosa Pinto, Ademir formed an attacking combination that terrorised the hapless opponents of Brazil.

Ademir kicked off with two goals in the opening match, including the first goal of the tournament, during a 4-0 victory over Mexico. Another goal followed in the 2-0 win over Yugoslavia.

When the hosts entered the final round amidst euphoric expectations of the football-crazy nation, Ademir cut loose, scoring four times in the 7-1 rout of Sweden. He scored again, once, in the 6-1 demolition of Spain that followed.

However, the run dried up tragically in the *Maracanazo*, the final game which went down as a national tragedy, when Uruguay pipped the hosts at the finishing post by winning 2-1.

Ademir also scored 18 goals in the 13 matches he played in the Copa América. It was to counter his brilliance that Brazillian club coaches had to introduce the fourth defender.

Inside-right Zizinho missed the first two matches due to an injury, refusing injections because he had a phobia of needles. But he did enough in the remaining games to be adjudged best player of the tournament. He scored just twice, but also had two goals disallowed in the match against Yugoslavia.

Zizinho was idolised by a young Pelé who considered him the best player he ever saw.

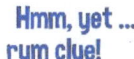

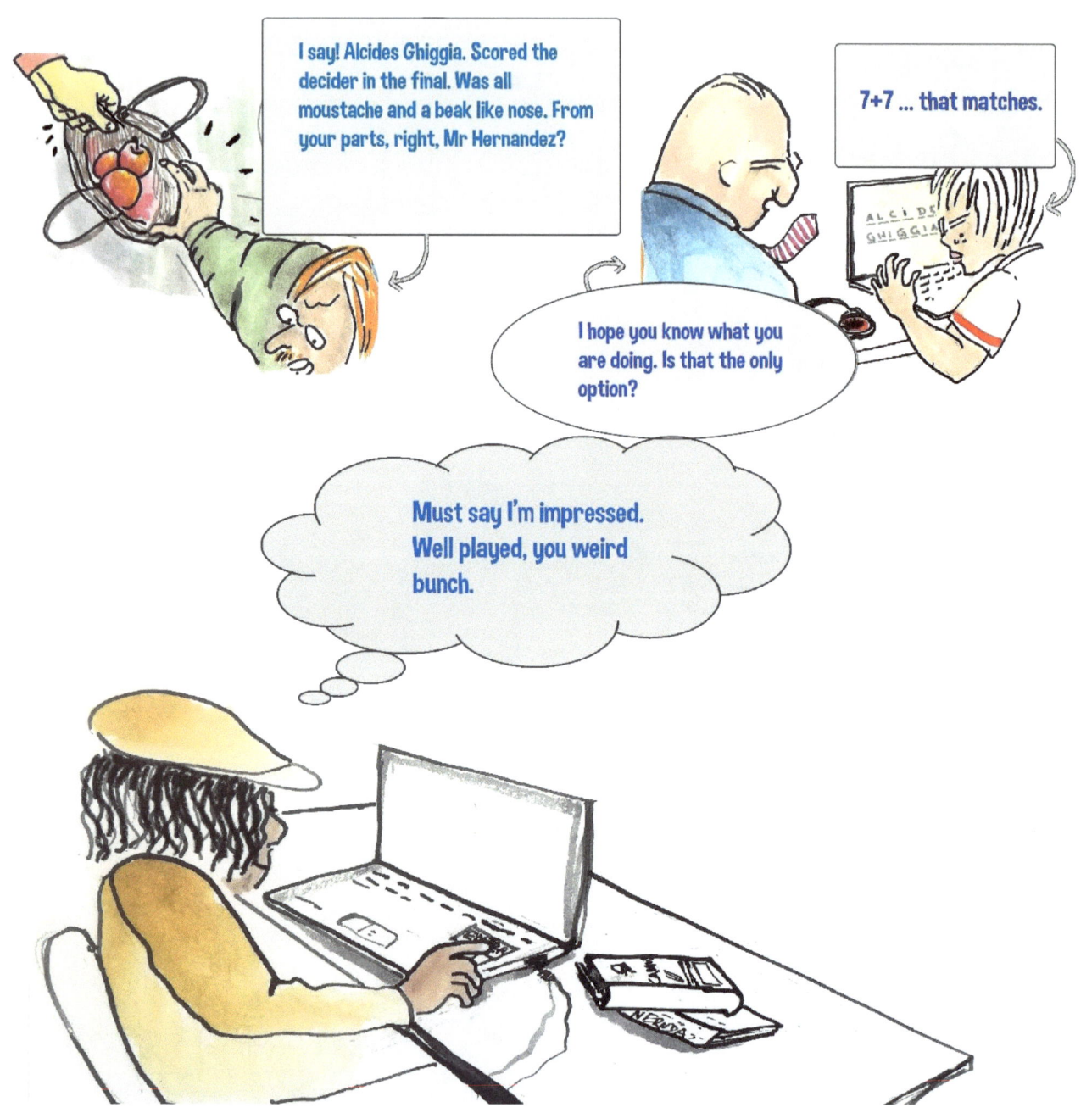

Correct. You have recovered the first 20% of your funds. This amount is being transferred back to your bank.

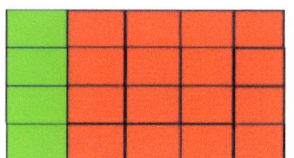

PHEW !

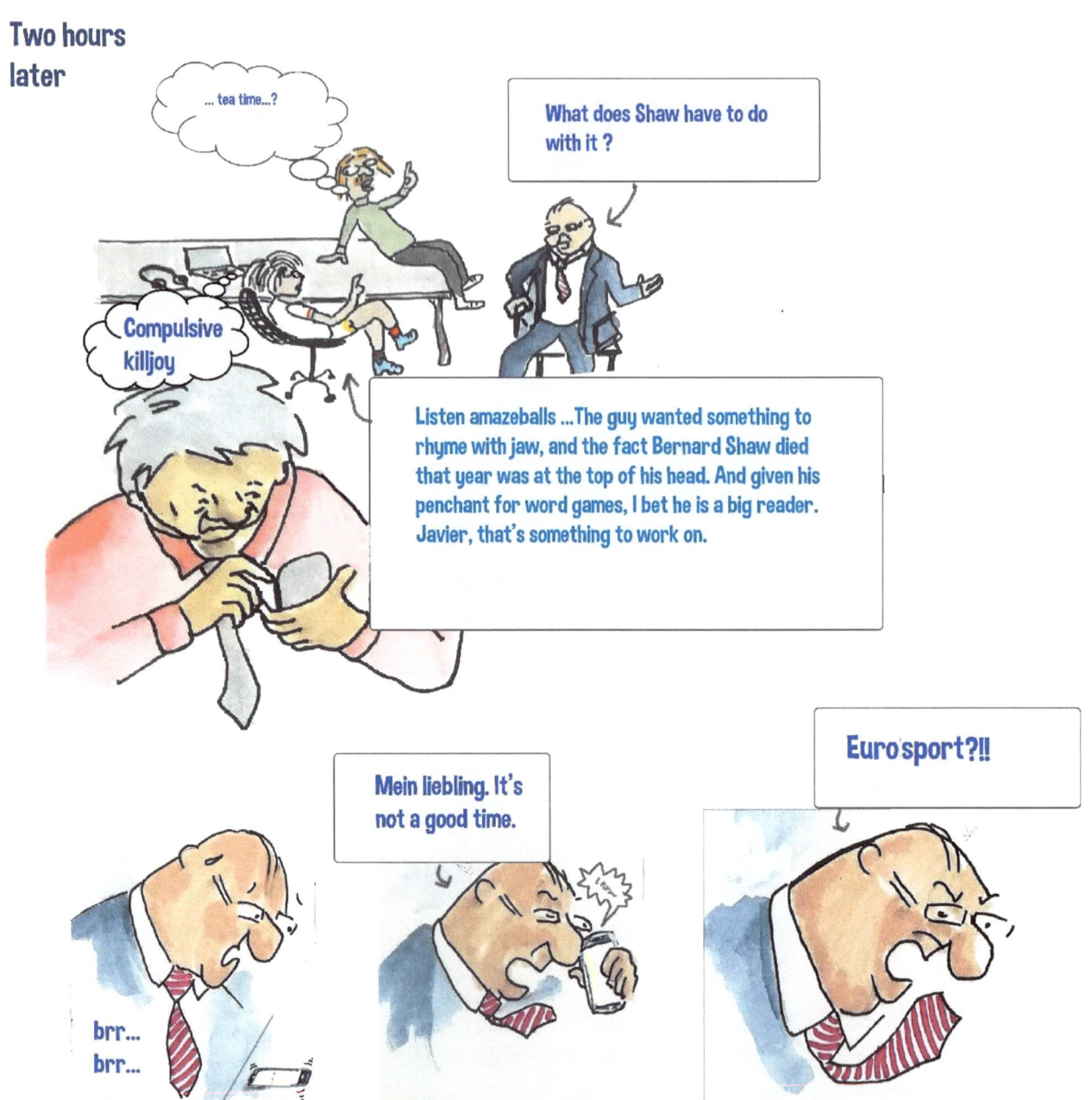

Can the team crack this cryptic puzzle? Can they recover the rest of the money?
Or will the World Cup be in jeopardy?

Who is this curious adversary they are up against? Will he play fair?
To find out more you must read the next volumes of SUDDEN DEATH

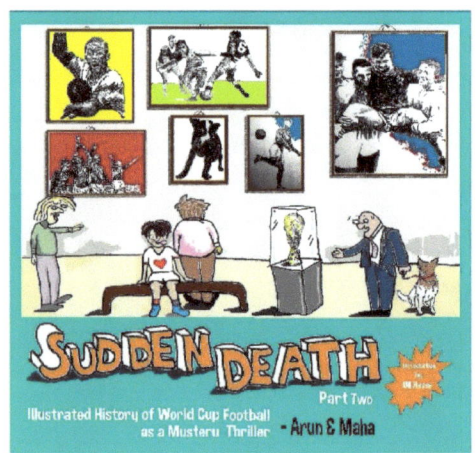

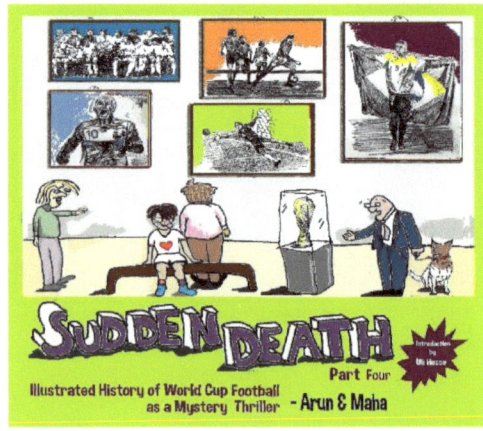

A Product of the Blinders team

www.ingramcontent.com/pod-product-compliance
Lightning Source LLC
LaVergne TN
LVHW072117070426
835510LV00003B/102